afternoon tea

afternoon tea

the taste of perfection

First published in 2011
LOVE FOOD is an imprint of Parragon Books Ltd

Parragon Publishing
Queen Street House
4 Queen Street
Bath BA1 1HE, UK

ISBN: 978-1-4454-2880-2

Printed in China

Introduction by Linda Doeser

Notes for the Reader
This book uses imperial, metric, and US cup measurements. Follow the same units of measurement
throughout; do not mix imperial and metric. All spoon measurements are level: teaspoons are assumed
to be 5 ml, and tablespoons are assumed to be 15 ml. Unless otherwise stated, milk is assumed to be
whole, eggs and individual vegetables, such as potatoes, are medium, and pepper is freshly ground
black pepper.

The times given are an approximate guide only. Preparation times differ according to the techniques used
by different people and the cooking times may also vary from those given as a result of the type of oven
used. Optional ingredients, variations, or serving suggestions have not been included in the calculations.

Recipes using raw or very lightly cooked eggs should be avoided by infants, the elderly, pregnant
women, convalescents, and anyone with a chronic condition. Pregnant and breast-feeding women are
advised to avoid eating peanuts and peanut products. People with nut allergies should be aware that
some of the prepared ingredients used in the recipes in this book may contain nuts. Always check the
package before use.

Contents

Afternoon Tea

Teatime is a quintessentially British ritual that perfectly mirrors the story of Britain's quirky class system. Afternoon tea—served between four and five o'clock—had nothing to do with hunger and everything to do with status and leisure. After a busy morning writing invitations and an exhausting afternoon choosing a new hat, the lady of the house would return to her drawing room, where she and her visitors could relax with delicate sandwiches cut into fingers or triangles, thin slices of bread and butter, and an array of tempting cakes and rich pastries. As they sipped their Earl Grey tea, poured into fragile porcelain cups from a silver teapot, they could eye each other's hats—only house guests would not wear one—and gossip happily. Gentlemen would sometimes be present and the younger ones would make themselves useful handing around cups, lifting the silver kettle from its stand, and surreptitiously flirting with the older daughters of the house. The children would have their own nursery tea elsewhere. Given that the day had already included both breakfast and luncheon, and a dinner of at least four courses was to follow, and that it was considered courteous for visitors to leave quite promptly, most of this lavish spread was often left untouched.

Tea for manual workers and agricultural laborers was quite a different kind of repast. They would sit at the table between five and six o'clock, together with their children, and enjoy high tea, having eaten their dinner at noon. The menu usually included a filling hot dish in the winter, such as herrings in oatmeal, and cold meat and salad in summer, consumed with plenty of bread and butter—but not in wafer-thin slices—followed by homemade cake. All this would be "washed down" with numerous cups of strong Indian tea.

Tea for the "middle" classes, as might be expected, was something of a mix of the two. Having eaten lunch, not luncheon, at one o'clock, they would have high tea on weekdays, often featuring a variety of teacakes, fancy cakes, and scones, but aspired to afternoon tea at weekends, especially Sundays. This required the best china and may even account for the rapid growth in the electroplating industry, as ambitious and sometimes snobbish hostesses regarded a china teapot as "not the done thing."

The decline of teatime

Like all customs, teatime changed over the years but it hung on in some form or another for much longer than might have been expected. Many formerly wealthy households experienced a drastic decline in income in the years following World War I, with a consequential dwindling of the number of servants and a reduction in their extravagant lifestyle. Young wives who had grown up in the 1920s wanted to run their homes in new ways

and abandoned the stuffy customs of their mothers. Cocktail hour became the society hostess's favorite time. In contrast, the middle classes developed the tea dance. Grand hotels served formal afternoon tea while an orchestra played foxtrots and quicksteps for light-footed patrons. World War II not only put an end to domestic service, except for the very rich, but also saw a massive growth in the female workforce. A cup of tea and a bun—a sweetened bread roll—at a tea shop was the nearest "office girls" came to afternoon tea, but many families still ate high tea even as late as the 1960s.

The "swinging sixties" brought huge changes to British society, including the availability of cheap foreign travel that introduced the insular British to other cuisines, none of which included teatime but most of which featured a glass of wine with dinner. Young people no longer lived in the family home until they got married but led independent lives in shared apartments with far too much going on in their exciting young world to stop for tea. School cooking lessons, which had always featured those perennial favorites, rock cakes, and strawberry sponge cake, were discontinued and takeout pizzas and supermarket prepared meals gradually superseded home cooking in many families.

Completing the circle

In the twenty-first century, with the fashion for grazing rather than family meals, televisions, computers, and game consoles in every room, and a population that is always running to catch up with itself, it looked as if afternoon tea had become an archaic ritual. Yet it has enjoyed a tremendous revival. Few, if any, still live the life of *Gosford Park*, but nostalgia for a more gracious and leisured way of life has grown. Fashionable "ladies who lunch" have switched their allegiance to meeting for tea at exclusive hotels. The tea dance was tentatively revived and has proved immensely popular, not just with those who can remember it but with a younger generation, too. The community-minded, who may not be able to afford to throw a grand fund-raising dinner, invite people into their homes for afternoon tea to raise money for their pet charities. On a more direct level, people who nowadays often live far away from their own families have joined groups that take turns to invite the elderly and isolated to tea. Where once it was considered modern to rip out fireplaces and board up chimneys, it is now the vogue to open them up again— and what could be nicer on a chilly Sunday afternoon than to snuggle cozily in front of a log fire with toast and pâté, scones and jam, and a plate of chocolate éclairs, even if the tea you're drinking is made with a tea bag in a mug rather than leaves in a silver pot?

Sandwiches and Snacks

Fancy Sandwiches

Makes 24 of each

shrimp salad pinwheels
- 3 tbsp cream cheese
- 4 oz/115 g fresh shrimp, mashed
- 1 stalk celery, finely chopped
- 1 tbsp mayonnaise
- lemon juice, to taste
- 6 slices white bread
- unsalted butter, softened
- salt and white pepper

deviled egg triangles
- 4 hard boiled large eggs, shelled and finely chopped
- 2 tbsp mayonnaise
- 1 tsp Dijon mustard
- pinch cayenne pepper
- unsalted butter, softened
- 12 slices whole-wheat bread
- salt and pepper

tuna salad round sandwiches
- 7 oz/200 g tuna in oil
- 3 tbsp mayonnaise
- finely grated rind of 1 lemon
- unsalted butter, softened
- 24 thin slices whole-grain bread
- fresh parsley, finely chopped
- salt and pepper

1 To make the shrimp salad filling, put the cheese in a bowl and beat until smooth. Stir the shrimp into the cheese with the celery and mayonnaise. Add the lemon juice and salt and white pepper to taste. Trim the crusts off the bread and cut each slice into rectangles about 3 x 5½ inch/7.5 x 13 cm. Flatten each slice with a rolling pin. Use your fingers to press two slices together at the short ends, squeezing to seal the seam; repeat to make three more long slices. Very lightly spread the slices with butter, then top with the shrimp mixture, taking it to the edges. Working with one long slice at a time, tightly roll up the bread, starting at a short end; repeat with the remaining three long slices. Wrap each slice very tightly in plastic wrap and chill for at least 1 hour. When ready to serve, remove from the refrigerator and use a serrated knife to thinly slice off both ends to neaten, then cut eight slices from each roll.

2 To make the deviled egg filling, put the eggs in a bowl, add the mayonnaise, mustard, and cayenne pepper and stir together. Add salt and pepper to taste. Spread the butter over the bread and spread the deviled egg mixture over six of the slices. Top with the remaining bread slices, buttered sides down. Use a serrated knife to cut off the crusts, then cut each sandwich into four triangles. Wrap tightly in plastic wrap and chill until ready to serve.

3 To make the tuna salad, flake the tuna into a bowl and beat in the mayonnaise until well blended. Stir in the lemon rind and salt and pepper to taste. Spread the butter over the bread slices. Use a 2-inch/5-cm round cutter to cut two circles from each slice. Spread the tuna mixture over 24 of the circles, then top with the remaining 24 circles, buttered sides down. Use a knife to neaten the edges, then spread very lightly with butter. Roll the buttered edges in the parsley. Stack the sandwiches, then wrap very tightly in plastic wrap and chill until ready to serve.

Cheese & Sun-Dried Tomato Toasts

Serves 4

- 2 small French loaves
- ¾ cup sun-dried tomato paste
- 1 small ball fresh buffalo mozzarella
- 1½ tsp dried oregano
- 2–3 tbsp olive oil
- pepper

1 Preheat the broiler to medium–high and preheat the oven to 425°F/220°C. Slice the loaves diagonally and discard the end pieces. Toast the slices on both sides under the broiler until golden.

2 Spread one side of each toast with the sun-dried tomato paste and top with mozzarella. Sprinkle with oregano and season to taste with pepper.

3 Put the toasts on a large baking sheet and drizzle with the oil. Bake in the preheated oven for 5 minutes, or until the cheese is melted and bubbling. Remove the toasts from the oven and let stand for 5 minutes before serving.

Crab Cake Toasts

Serves 2-4

- 3 slices white bread, crusts removed
- 2 tbsp milk
- 2 tbsp butter, melted
- 5 oz/140 g frozen crabmeat, thawed
- 1 green chile, seeded and chopped
- 1 scallion, finely chopped
- salt and pepper
- lemon wedges, to garnish

1 Place one piece of bread on a plate and spoon the milk evenly over it. Let stand for a few minutes. Brush the remaining slices lightly on both sides with some of the butter.

2 Mix the crabmeat, chile, and scallion in a bowl. Mash the soaked bread with a fork and mix it with the crabmeat, scraping in the milk off the plate. Stir in the remaining melted butter and season to taste.

3 Preheat the broiler to medium–high and toast the buttered bread until crisp and golden on both sides. Top with the crab mixture, spreading it evenly right to the edges, and forking the surface slightly so that it is not too smooth.

4 Place under the broiler for about 3 minutes, until the creamy topping is browned. Serve at once, garnished with lemon wedges so that their juices can be squeezed over the crab.

Smoked Salmon Blinis

Makes 24

- ⅓ cup sour cream
- finely grated rind of 2 lemons
- 3 tbsp finely snipped fresh chives, plus extra pieces to garnish
- 2 oz/55 g smoked salmon, finely sliced
- pepper

blinis

- ⅔ cup all-purpose flour
- 1 tsp active dry yeast
- ½ tsp sugar
- ⅔ cup warm water
- ¾ cup buckwheat flour
- ½ cup warm milk
- 3 tbsp butter, melted and cooled
- 1 large egg, separated
- vegetable oil, for cooking
- salt and pepper

1 To make the blinis, stir together the all-purpose flour, yeast, and sugar in a bowl. Make a well in the center and slowly add the water, drawing in the flour from the side to make a wet, lumpy batter. Beat until the batter is smooth, then stir in the buckwheat flour, cover the bowl tightly with a dish towel, and set aside for 1 hour, until the batter has risen and the surface is covered with air bubbles.

2 Meanwhile, mix the sour cream with the lemon rind, chives, and pepper to taste. Cover and chill until ready to use.

3 Stir together the milk, butter, egg yolk, and a generous pinch of salt and pepper, then add to the batter, stirring well until blended. Beat the egg white in a separate bowl until soft peaks form, and then fold into the batter.

4 Heat a large skillet over medium heat until you can feel the heat rising, then lightly brush the surface all over with vegetable oil using a crumpled paper towel. Fill a tablespoon measure two-thirds full with the batter, then drop the batter onto the hot surface so it forms a circle about 2 inches/5 cm across; add as many more as will fit in the skillet without touching. Cook for just over a minute, or until the top surface is covered with air holes and the bottom is golden brown and set. Use a spatula to flip over the blinis and cook until set and golden brown. Transfer to a heatproof plate and keep warm in a low oven while you cook the remaining batter.

5 To serve, arrange the warm, not hot, blinis on a platter and top each with about 2 teaspoons of the chilled sour cream. Lay the salmon strips over the sour cream, add a little piece of chive to each, and serve.

Smoked Fish Pâté

Serves 8

- 2 lb/900 g smoked fish of your choice
- 2 garlic cloves, finely chopped
- ¾ cup olive oil
- 6 tbsp light cream
- salt and pepper
- lemon wedges and oatcakes or warm toast, to serve

1 Put the fish in a fish kettle or large skillet and add cold water to just cover. Bring to a boil, then immediately reduce the heat and poach gently for 10 minutes, until tender. If using a skillet, you may need to do this in batches.

2 Transfer the fish to a cutting board using a spatula. Remove and discard the skin. Roughly flake the flesh with a fork and remove and discard any remaining tiny bones. Transfer the fish to a saucepan over low heat, add the garlic, and break up the fish with a wooden spoon.

3 Gradually add the oil, beating well after each addition. Add the cream and beat until smooth, but do not let the mixture boil.

4 Remove the saucepan from the heat and season to taste with salt, if necessary, and pepper. Spoon the pâté into a serving dish, cover, and set aside to cool completely. Chill in the refrigerator until required for up to 3 days.

5 Serve with lemon wedges and oatcakes.

Cheese & Mustard Biscuits

Makes 8

- 4 tbsp butter, cut into small pieces, plus extra for greasing and to serve
- generous 1½ cups self-rising flour, plus extra for dusting
- 1 tsp baking powder
- pinch of salt
- 1½ cups grated sharp cheddar cheese plus extra, diced, to serve
- 1 tsp dry mustard
- ⅔ cup milk, plus extra for brushing
- pepper

1 Preheat the oven to 425°F/220°C. Lightly grease a baking sheet.

2 Sift the flour, baking powder, and salt into a mixing bowl. Rub in the butter with your fingertips until the mixture resembles breadcrumbs.

3 Stir in the cheese, mustard, and enough milk to form a soft dough.

4 On a lightly floured surface, knead the dough very lightly, then flatten it out with the palm of your hand to a depth of about 1 inch/2.5 cm.

5 Cut the dough into eight wedges with a knife. Brush each one with a little milk and sprinkle with pepper to taste.

6 Bake in the preheated oven for 10–15 minutes, until golden brown. Transfer the biscuits to a wire rack and let cool slightly before serving with cheese and butter.

Blue Cheese & Walnut Tartlets

Makes 6

walnut pie dough

- scant ½ cup (1 stick) cold butter, diced, plus extra for greasing
- generous 1½ cups all-purpose flour, plus extra for dusting
- pinch of celery salt
- ¼ cup chopped walnut halves
- ice-cold water

filling

- 2 tbsp butter
- 2 celery stalks, finely chopped
- 1 small leek, finely chopped
- generous 1 cup heavy cream
- 7 oz/200 g blue cheese
- 3 egg yolks
- salt and pepper

1 To make the dough, lightly grease a 3-inch/7.5-cm, 12-cup muffin pan. Sift the flour with the celery salt into a food processor, add the butter, and process until the mixture resembles breadcrumbs. Turn into a large bowl and add the walnuts and a little cold water, just enough to bring the dough together. Turn out onto a lightly floured surface and cut the dough in half. Roll out the first piece and cut out six 3½-inch/9-cm rounds.

2 Roll out each round to 4½ inches/12 cm in diameter and use to line the muffin cups. Repeat with the remaining dough. Line each hole with parchment paper and fill with pie weights or dried beans. Chill in the refrigerator for 30 minutes. Meanwhile, preheat the oven to 400°F/200°C.

3 Bake the tartlet shells for 10 minutes. Remove from the oven, then remove the paper and weights.

4 To make the filling, melt the butter in a skillet over medium–low heat, add the celery and leek, and cook, stirring occasionally, for 15 minutes, until very soft. Add 2 tablespoons of cream, crumble in the cheese, and mix well. Season to taste with salt and pepper. Put the remaining cream in a saucepan and bring to simmering point. Put the eggs into a bowl, then pour a cheese mixture over the eggs with the cream, and stir continuously.

5 Mix in the cheese mixture and spoon into the tartlet shells. Bake for 10 minutes, then turn the pan around in the oven and bake for an additional 5 minutes. Let the tartlets cool in the pan for 5 minutes before serving.

Leek & Onion Tartlets

Makes 6

pastry
- butter, for greasing
- 8 oz/225 g store-bought unsweetened pie dough
- all-purpose flour, for dusting

filling
- 2 tbsp unsalted butter
- 1 onion, thinly sliced
- 1 lb/450 g leeks, thinly sliced
- 2 tsp chopped fresh thyme
- ½ cup grated Gruyère cheese
- 3 eggs
- 1¼ cups heavy cream
- salt and pepper

1 Lightly grease six 4-inch/10-cm tartlet pans with butter. Roll out the dough on a lightly floured surface and stamp out 6 rounds with a 5-inch/13-cm cutter. Ease the dough into the pans, prick the bottoms, and chill for 30 minutes.

2 Preheat the oven to 375°F/190°C. Line the pastry shells with foil and pie weights or dried beans, then place on a baking sheet and bake for 8 minutes. Remove the foil and weights and bake for an additional 2 minutes. Transfer the pans to a wire rack to cool. Reduce the oven temperature to 350°F/180°C.

3 Meanwhile, make the filling. Melt the butter in a large, heavy-bottom skillet. Add the onion and cook, stirring continuously, for 5 minutes, or until softened. Add the leeks and thyme and cook, stirring, for 10 minutes, or until softened. Divide the leek mixture among the tartlet shells. Sprinkle with Gruyère cheese.

4 Lightly beat the eggs with the cream and season to taste with salt and pepper. Place the tartlet pans on a baking sheet and divide the egg mixture among them. Bake in the preheated oven for 15 minutes, or until the filling is set and golden brown. Transfer to a wire rack to cool slightly before removing from the pans and serving.

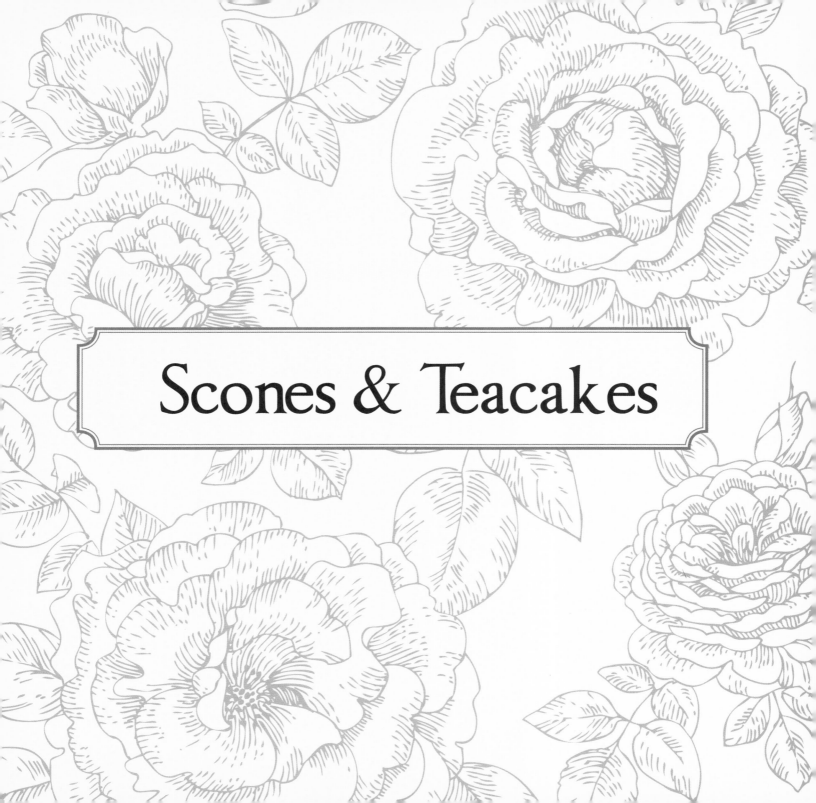

Scones & Teacakes

Traditional English Scones

Makes 10

- 3½ cups all-purpose flour, plus extra for dusting
- ½ tsp salt
- 2 tsp baking powder
- 4 tbsp butter
- 2 tbsp superfine sugar
- 1 cup milk
- 3 tbsp milk, for glazing
- strawberry preserves and whipped heavy cream, to serve

1 Preheat the oven to 425°F/220°C. Sift the flour, salt, and baking powder into a bowl. Rub in the butter until the mixture resembles breadcrumbs. Stir in the sugar. Make a well in the center and pour in the milk. Stir in using a palette knife and make a soft dough.

2 Turn the dough onto a lightly floured surface and lightly flatten until it is of an even thickness, about ½ inch/1 cm. Use a 2½-inch/6-cm cookie cutter to cut out the dough and place on the baking sheet. Glaze with a little milk and bake for 10–12 minutes, until golden and well risen.

3 Cool on a wire rack and serve freshly baked with strawberry preserves and whipped heavy cream.

Orange & Banana Scones

Makes 12

- sunflower oil, for oiling
- generous 1 cup white self-rising flour, plus extra for dusting
- heaping 1 cup whole-wheat self-rising flour
- 1 tsp baking powder
- ½ tsp ground cinnamon
- generous 5½ tbsp unsalted butter, diced and chilled
- ¼ cup packed brown sugar
- ⅔ cup whole milk, plus extra for brushing
- 1 ripe banana, peeled and mashed
- finely grated rind of 1 orange
- 1¼ cups fresh raspberries, lightly mashed

1 Preheat the oven to 400°F/200°C. Lightly oil a large baking sheet.

2 Mix the flours, baking powder, and cinnamon together in a large bowl, add the butter, and rub in with your fingertips until the mixture resembles breadcrumbs. Stir in the sugar. Make a well in the center and pour in the milk. Add the banana and orange rind, and mix to a soft dough. The dough will be wet.

3 Turn out the dough onto a lightly floured surface and, adding a little more flour if needed, roll out to ¾ inch/2 cm thick. Using a 2½-inch/6-cm cookie cutter, cut out 12 scones, rerolling the trimmings where possible, and place them on the prepared baking sheet. Brush with milk and bake in the preheated oven for 10–12 minutes.

4 Remove from the oven and let cool slightly, then halve the scones and fill with the raspberries.

Cherry & Golden Raisin Scones

Makes 8

- 6 tbsp butter, cut into small pieces, plus extra for greasing
- generous 1¾ cups self-rising flour, plus extra for dusting
- 1 tbsp superfine sugar
- pinch of salt
- 3 tbsp chopped candied cherries
- 3 tbsp golden raisins
- 1 egg, lightly beaten
- 2 tbsp milk, plus extra for brushing

1 Preheat the oven to 425°F/220°C. Grease a baking sheet and line with parchment paper.

2 Sift the flour, sugar, and salt into a mixing bowl and rub in the butter with your fingertips until the mixture resembles breadcrumbs.

3 Stir in the candied cherries and golden raisins. Add the egg and the milk and mix well together to form a soft dough.

4 On a lightly floured surface, roll out the dough to a thickness of ¾ inch/2 cm, and cut out eight rounds using a 2-inch/5-cm round cutter.

5 Place the rounds on the prepared baking sheet and brush the tops with milk.

6 Bake in the preheated oven for 8–10 minutes, or until the scones are golden brown. Transfer to a wire rack to cool completely.

Tea Cakes

Makes 10-12

- 1¼ cups milk
- 4 tsp active dry yeast
- ¼ cup superfine sugar
- 3⅓ cups white bread flour, plus extra for dusting
- 1 tsp salt
- 1 tsp ground allspice
- ¾ cup currants
- 2 tbsp chopped candied peel
- 4 tbsp butter, melted plus extra for greasing
- 1 egg, beaten
- sugar glaze made from 2 tbsp sugar and 2 tbsp warm milk

1 Warm the milk in a saucepan until just tepid and add the yeast with 1 teaspoon of the sugar. Mix well and let froth in a warm place for 15 minutes.

2 Sift the flour, salt, and allspice into a large mixing bowl and add the currants, peel, and the remaining sugar. Make a well in the center of the dry ingredients and pour in the milk mixture, the melted butter, and the egg. Mix well using a wooden spoon at first and then by hand. Turn out onto a lightly floured surface and knead lightly until the dough is smooth and elastic.

3 Put the dough back into the bowl, cover with plastic wrap, and let stand to rise in a warm place for 40–45 minutes, until it has doubled in size. Knead the dough again lightly and divide into 10–12 even rolls, shaping well.

4 Preheat the oven to 425°F/220°C. Place the rolls on two greased baking sheets, cover with a damp dish towel or large plastic bags, and let stand to rise again for 30–40 minutes. Bake the fruit rolls in the oven for 18–20 minutes, until they are golden brown. Remove from the oven, place on a wire rack, and glaze with the sugar glaze while still hot.

Eccles Cakes

Makes 10-12

- 4 tbsp butter, softened
- 14 oz/400 g store-bought puff pastry
- 2 tbsp all-purpose flour, for dusting
- ¼ cup brown sugar
- ½ cup currants
- ¼ cup chopped mixed candied citrus peel
- ½ tsp ground allspice (optional)
- 1 egg white, lightly beaten
- 1 tsp superfine sugar

1 Preheat the oven to 425°F/220°C and grease a baking sheet. Roll out the pastry thinly on a lightly floured surface using a rolling pin. Cut into rounds using a 3½-inch/9-cm cutter. Fold the trimmings carefully, reroll, and cut again to make a total of 10–12 rounds.

2 In a bowl, mix together the butter and brown sugar until creamy, then add the dried fruit and allspice, if using.

3 Put a teaspoon of the filing in the center of each pastry round. Draw the edges of the circles together and pinch the edges over the filling. Reshape each cake into a round. Turn the cakes over and lightly roll them with the rolling pin until the currants just show through. Score with a knife into a lattice pattern. Place on the prepared baking sheet and let rest for 10–15 minutes.

4 Brush the cakes with the egg white, sprinkle with the superfine sugar, and bake at the top of the preheated oven for about 15 minutes until golden brown and crisp.

5 Transfer to a wire rack and sprinkle with a little more sugar if desired. Serve immediately, or store in an airtight container for up to a week and reheat before serving.

Brioche

Serves 6

- 2 cups white bread flour,
  plus extra for dusting
- ½ tsp salt
- 1 tbsp superfine sugar
- 1½ tsp active dry yeast
- 2 eggs
- 2 tbsp lukewarm milk
- 4 tbsp unsalted butter, softened,
  plus extra for greasing

glaze
- 1 egg yolk
- 1 tbsp milk

1 Sift the flour and salt into a food processor and add the sugar and yeast. Lightly beat the eggs with the milk in a bowl. With the machine running, gradually add the egg-and-milk mixture and process, scraping down the sides as necessary, for 2–3 minutes, until a dough forms. Cut the butter into small pieces and add to the dough. Pulse the machine until the butter is completely incorporated.

2 Grease a bowl with butter. Shape the dough into a ball, put it into the bowl, and put the bowl into a plastic bag or cover with a damp dish towel. Let rise in a warm place for 1 hour, until the dough has doubled in volume.

3 Grease a brioche mold with butter. Turn out the dough onto a lightly floured surface and punch down gently with your fist. Cut off about one-quarter of the dough and wrap in plastic wrap. Knead the larger piece of dough, shape into a ball, place in the prepared mold, and indent the top. Unwrap the smaller piece of dough, knead lightly into a pear shape, and place on top of the indent to make the "tête."

4 Put the mold into a plastic bag or cover with a damp dish towel and let rise in a warm place for 1 hour.

5 Preheat the oven to 425°F/220°C. To make the glaze, beat the egg yolk with the milk, then brush over the top of the brioche. Bake for 40–45 minutes, until golden brown. Turn out onto a wire rack to cool.

Strawberry Jam

makes about 1½ cups

- 3 lb 5 oz/1.5 kg ripe, unblemished whole strawberries, hulled and rinsed
- 2 freshly squeezed lemons, juice strained
- 7½ cups sugar (about 3 lb 5 oz/1.5 kg)
- 1 tsp butter

1 Place the strawberries in a large pan with the lemon juice, then simmer over gentle heat for 15–20 minutes, stirring occasionally, until the fruit has collapsed and is very soft.

2 Add the sugar and heat, stirring occasionally, until the sugar has completely dissolved. Add the butter, then bring to a boil and boil rapidly for 10–20 minutes, or until the setting point is reached.

3 Let cool for 8–10 minutes, then skim. Pot into warmed sterilized jars and cover the tops with wax disks. When completely cold, cover with cellophane or lids, then label and store in a cool place.

Orange Marmalade

makes about 14 cups
- 3 lb 5 oz/1.5 kg Seville oranges, scrubbed
- juice from 2 large lemons
- 24 cups water
- 13½ cups sugar (about 6 lb/ 2.7 kg)

1 Cut the oranges in half and squeeze out all the juice. Scoop out all the seeds from the orange shells and tie up in a small piece of cheesecloth. Slice the peel into small chunks or strips and place in a large pan together with the orange and lemon juice and water. Add the bag of seeds.

2 Simmer gently for 1½ hours, or until the peel is very soft and the liquid has reduced by half. Remove the bag of seeds, carefully squeezing to remove any juices. Add the sugar and heat, stirring until the sugar has completely dissolved. Bring to a boil and boil rapidly for about 15 minutes, or until the setting point is reached.

3 Let cool slightly, then pot into warmed sterilized jars and cover the tops with wax disks. When completely cold, cover with cellophane or lids, then label and store in a cool place.

Little & Large Cakes

Strawberry Sponge Cake

Serves 8

- ¾ cup (1½ sticks) butter, softened, plus extra for greasing
- 1¼ cups self-rising flour
- 1 tsp baking powder
- scant 1 cup superfine sugar
- 3 eggs
- confectioners' sugar, for dusting

filling

- 3 tbsp raspberry jam
- 1¼ cups heavy cream, whipped
- 16 fresh strawberries, halved

1 Preheat the oven to 350°F/180°C, then grease and line the bottoms of two 8-inch/20-cm round layer cake pans.

2 Sift the flour and baking powder into a bowl and add the butter, superfine sugar, and eggs. Mix together, then beat well until smooth.

3 Divide the dough evenly between the prepared pans and smooth the surfaces. Bake in the preheated oven for 25–30 minutes, or until well risen and golden brown, and the cakes feel springy when lightly pressed.

4 Let cool in the pans for 5 minutes, then transfer to wire racks to cool completely. Sandwich the cakes together with the raspberry jam, whipped heavy cream, and strawberry halves. Dust with confectioners' sugar and serve.

Rich Fruitcake

Serves 16

- scant 2½ cups golden raisins
- 1⅔ cups raisins
- ½ cup chopped dried apricots
- ½ cup chopped pitted dates
- 4 tbsp dark rum or brandy, plus extra for flavoring (optional)
- finely grated rind and juice of 1 orange
- 1 cup (2 sticks) butter, plus extra for greasing
- 1 cup light brown sugar
- 4 eggs
- generous ⅓ cup chopped candied peel
- ⅓ cup quartered candied cherries
- 2 tbsp chopped candied ginger or preserved ginger
- ⅓ cup chopped blanched almonds
- 1¾ cups all-purpose flour
- 1 tsp apple pie spice

1 Place the golden raisins, raisins, apricots, and dates in a large bowl and stir in the rum, orange rind, and orange juice. Cover and let soak for several hours or overnight.

2 Preheat the oven to 300°F/150°C. Grease and line an 8-inch/20-cm round deep cake pan.

3 Cream together the butter and sugar until light and fluffy. Gradually beat in the eggs, beating hard after each addition. Stir in the soaked fruits, candied peel, candied cherries, candied ginger, and blanched almonds.

4 Sift together the flour and apple pie spice, then fold lightly and evenly into the mixture. Spoon into the prepared cake pan and level the surface, making a slight depression in the center with the back of the spoon.

5 Bake in the preheated oven for 2¼–2¾ hours, or until the cake is beginning to shrink away from the sides of the pan and a toothpick inserted into the center comes out clean. Cool completely in the pan.

6 Turn out the cake and remove the lining paper. Wrap with wax paper and foil and store for at least 2 months before use. To add a richer flavor, prick the cake with a toothpick and spoon over a couple of tablespoons of rum or brandy, if using, before storing.

Coffee & Walnut Cake

Serves 8

- ¾ cup (1½ sticks) butter, plus extra for greasing
- ¾ cup light brown sugar
- 3 extra-large eggs, beaten
- 3 tbsp strong black coffee
- 1½ cups self-rising flour
- 1½ tsp baking powder
- 1 cup walnut pieces
- walnut halves, to decorate

frosting
- ½ cup (1 stick) butter
- 1¾ cups confectioners' sugar
- 1 tbsp strong black coffee
- ½ tsp vanilla extract

1 Preheat the oven to 350°F/180°C. Grease and line the bottoms of two 8-inch/20-cm round layer cake pans.

2 Cream together the butter and brown sugar until pale and fluffy. Gradually add the eggs, beating well after each addition. Beat in the coffee.

3 Sift the flour and baking powder into the mixture, then fold in lightly and evenly with a metal spoon. Fold in the walnut pieces.

4 Divide the batter between the prepared cake pans and smooth level. Bake in the preheated oven for 20–25 minutes, or until golden brown and springy to the touch. Turn out onto a wire rack to cool.

5 For the frosting, beat together the butter, confectioners' sugar, coffee, and vanilla extract, mixing until smooth and creamy.

6 Use about half of the frosting to sandwich the cakes together, then spread the remaining frosting on top and swirl with a metal spatula. Decorate with the walnut halves.

Frosted Carrot Cake

Serves 16

- ¾ cup sunflower oil, plus extra for greasing
- ¾ cup light brown sugar
- 3 eggs, beaten
- 1¾ cups grated carrots
- ⅔ cup golden raisins
- ½ cup walnut pieces
- grated rind of 1 orange
- 1½ cups self-rising flour
- 1 tsp baking soda
- 1 tsp ground cinnamon
- ½ tsp grated nutmeg
- strips of orange zest, to decorate

frosting

- scant 1 cup cream cheese
- scant 1 cup confectioners' sugar
- 2 tsp orange juice

1 Preheat the oven to 350°F/180°C. Grease a 9-inch/23-cm square cake pan and line the bottom with parchment paper.

2 In a large bowl, beat the oil, brown sugar, and eggs together. Stir in the carrots, golden raisins, walnuts, and orange rind.

3 Sift together the flour, baking soda, cinnamon, and nutmeg, then stir into the carrot mixture.

4 Spoon the batter into the prepared cake pan and bake in the preheated oven for 40–45 minutes, until well risen and firm to the touch.

5 Remove the cake from the oven and set on a wire rack for 5 minutes. Turn out onto the wire rack to cool completely.

6 For the frosting, combine the cream cheese, confectioners' sugar, and orange juice in a bowl and beat until smooth. Spread over the cake and swirl with a spatula. Decorate with strips of orange zest and serve cut into squares.

Lemon Drizzle Cake

Serves 12

- ⅔ cup soft margarine, plus extra for greasing
- 2 eggs
- generous ¾ cup superfine sugar
- finely grated rind of 1 lemon
- 1½ cups self-rising flour
- ½ cup milk
- confectioners' sugar, for dusting

syrup
- 1¼ cups confectioners' sugar
- ¼ cup fresh lemon juice

1 Preheat the oven to 350°F/180°C. Grease a 7-inch/18-cm square cake pan and line with nonstick parchment paper.

2 Place the eggs, superfine sugar, and margarine in a bowl and beat hard until smooth and fluffy. Stir in the lemon rind, then fold in the flour lightly and evenly. Stir in the milk, mixing evenly, then spoon into the prepared cake pan, smoothing level.

3 Bake in the preheated oven for 45–50 minutes, or until golden brown and firm to the touch. Remove from the oven and place the pan on a wire rack.

4 To make the syrup, place the confectioners' sugar and lemon juice in a small saucepan and heat gently, stirring until the sugar dissolves. Do not boil.

5 Prick the warm cake all over with a skewer and spoon the hot syrup evenly over the top.

6 Let cool completely in the pan, then turn out the cake, cut into 12 pieces, and dust with a little confectioners' sugar before serving.

Pound Cake

Serves 8-10

- ¾ cup (1½ sticks) unsalted butter, plus extra for greasing
- scant 1 cup superfine sugar
- finely grated rind of 1 lemon
- 3 extra-large eggs, beaten
- 1 cup all-purpose flour
- 1 cup self-rising flour
- 2–3 tbsp brandy or milk
- 2 slices of citrus peel

1 Preheat the oven to 325°F/160°C. Grease and line a 7-inch/18-cm round deep cake pan.

2 Cream together the butter and sugar until pale and fluffy. Add the lemon rind and gradually beat in the eggs. Sift in the flours and fold in evenly, adding enough brandy to make a soft consistency.

3 Spoon the batter into the prepared pan and smooth the surface. Lay the slices of citron peel on top of the cake.

4 Bake in the preheated oven for 1–1¼ hours, or until well risen, golden brown, and springy to the touch.

5 Cool in the pan for 10 minutes, then turn out and cool completely on a wire rack.

Vanilla Frosted Cupcakes

Makes 12

- ½ cup (1 stick) unsalted butter, softened
- generous ½ cup superfine sugar
- 2 eggs, lightly beaten
- ¾ cup self-rising flour
- 1 tbsp milk
- candied rose petals, to decorate

frosting

- ¾ cup (1½ stick) unsalted butter, softened
- 2 tsp vanilla extract
- 2 tbsp milk
- scant 2⅔ cups confectioners' sugar, sifted

1 Preheat the oven to 350°F/180°C. Put 12 paper liners in a 12-cup muffin pan.

2 Place the butter and sugar in a bowl and beat together until light and fluffy. Gradually beat in the eggs. Sift in the flour and fold in gently using a metal spoon. Fold in the milk.

3 Spoon the batter into the paper liners. Bake in the preheated oven for 15–20 minutes, until golden brown and firm to the touch. Transfer to a wire rack and let cool.

4 To make the frosting, put the butter, vanilla extract, and milk in a large bowl. Using a handheld mixer, beat the mixture until smooth. Gradually beat in the confectioners' sugar and continue beating for 2–3 minutes, until the frosting is light and creamy.

5 Spoon the frosting into a large pastry bag fitted with a large star tip and pipe swirls of the frosting onto the top of each cupcake. Decorate each cupcake with candied rose petals.

Gingerbread Cupcakes

Makes 16

- generous ¾ cup all-purpose flour
- 2 tsp ground ginger
- ¾ tsp ground cinnamon
- 1 piece of preserved ginger, chopped
- ¾ tsp baking soda
- 4 tbsp milk
- 6 tbsp butter, softened
- generous ⅓ cup firmly packed brown sugar
- 2 tbsp molasses
- 2 eggs, lightly beaten
- pieces of preserved ginger, finely chopped, to decorate

frosting

- 6 tbsp butter, softened
- 1½ cups confectioners' sugar
- 2 tbsp ginger syrup from the preserved ginger jar

1 Preheat the oven to 325°F/160°C. Put 16 paper liners in two muffin pans or put 16 double-layer paper liners on two baking sheets.

2 Sift the flour, ground ginger, and cinnamon together into a bowl. Add the chopped ginger and toss in the flour mixture until well coated. In a separate bowl, dissolve the baking soda in the milk.

3 Put the butter and sugar in a bowl and beat together until fluffy. Beat in the molasses, then gradually add the eggs, beating well after each addition. Beat in the flour mixture, then gradually beat in the milk. Spoon the batter into the paper liners.

4 Bake the cupcakes in the preheated oven for 20 minutes, or until well risen and golden brown. Transfer to a wire rack and let cool.

5 To make the frosting, put the butter in a bowl and beat until fluffy. Sift in the confectioners' sugar, add the ginger syrup, and beat together until smooth and creamy.

6 When the cupcakes are cold, spread the frosting on top of each cupcake, then decorate with pieces of ginger.

Pastries & Fancy Desserts

Vanilla Macaroons

Makes 16

- ¾ cup ground almonds
- 1 cup confectioners' sugar
- 2 extra-large egg whites
- ¼ cup superfine sugar
- ½ tsp vanilla extract

filling

- 4 tbsp unsalted butter, softened
- ½ tsp vanilla extract
- 1 cup confectioners' sugar, sifted

1 Line two baking sheets with parchment paper. Place the ground almonds and confectioners' sugar in a food processor and process for 15 seconds. Sift the mixture into a bowl.

2 Place the egg whites in a large bowl and whip until holding soft peaks. Gradually beat in the superfine sugar to make a firm, glossy meringue. Beat in the vanilla extract.

3 Using a palette knife, fold the almond mixture into the meringue one-third at a time. When all the dry ingredients are thoroughly incorporated, continue to cut and fold the mixture until it forms a shiny batter with a thick, ribbonlike consistency.

4 Pour the batter into a pastry bag fitted with a ½-inch/1-cm plain tip. Pipe 32 small circles onto the prepared baking sheets. Tap the baking sheets firmly onto a work surface to remove air bubbles. Let stand at room temperature for 30 minutes. Preheat the oven to 325°F/160°C.

5 Bake in the preheated oven for 10–15 minutes. Cool for 10 minutes. Carefully peel the macaroons off the parchment paper and let cool completely.

6 To make the filling, beat the butter and vanilla extract in a bowl until pale and fluffy. Gradually beat in the confectioners' sugar until smooth and creamy. Use to sandwich pairs of macaroons together.

Chocolate Hazelnut Macaroons

Makes 16

- ½ cup ground almonds
- ¼ cup finely ground hazelnuts, plus 1 tbsp chopped, to decorate
- 1 cup confectioners' sugar
- 2 extra-large egg whites
- ¼ cup superfine sugar
- generous ⅓ cup hazelnut-and-chocolate spread

1 Line two baking sheets with parchment paper. Place the ground almonds, ground hazelnuts, and confectioners' sugar in a food processor and process for 15 seconds. Sift the mixture into a bowl.

2 Place the egg whites in a large bowl and whip until holding soft peaks. Gradually beat in the superfine sugar to make a firm, glossy meringue.

3 Using a palette knife, fold the almond mixture into the meringue one-third at a time. When all the dry ingredients are thoroughly incorporated, continue to cut and fold the mixture until it forms a shiny batter with a thick, ribbonlike consistency.

4 Pour the batter into a pastry bag fitted with a ½-inch/1-cm plain tip. Pipe 32 small circles onto the prepared baking sheets. Tap the baking sheets firmly onto a work surface to remove air bubbles. Sprinkle over the chopped hazelnuts. Let stand at room temperature for 30 minutes. Preheat the oven to 325°F/160°C.

5 Bake in the preheated oven for 10–15 minutes. Cool for 10 minutes. Carefully peel the macaroons off the parchment paper and let cool completely.

6 Sandwich pairs of macaroons together with the hazelnut-and-chocolate spread.

Mini Florentines

Makes 40

- 6 tbsp unsalted butter, plus extra for greasing
- all-purpose flour, for dusting
- 6 tbsp superfine sugar
- 2 tbsp golden raisins
- 2 tbsp chopped candied cherries
- 2 tbsp chopped preserved ginger
- 2½ tbsp sunflower seeds
- 1 cup slivered almonds
- 2 tbsp heavy cream
- 6 oz/175 g semisweet or milk chocolate, broken into pieces

1 Preheat the oven to 350°F/180°C. Grease and flour two baking sheets or line with parchment paper.

2 Place the butter in a small saucepan and heat gently until melted. Add the sugar, stir until dissolved, then bring the mixture to a boil. Remove from the heat and stir in the golden raisins, cherries, ginger, sunflower seeds, and almonds. Mix well, then beat in the cream.

3 Place small teaspoons of the fruit-and-nut mixture onto the prepared baking sheets, allowing plenty of room for the mixture to spread during baking. Bake in the preheated oven for 10–12 minutes, or until light golden in color.

4 Remove from the oven and, while still hot, use a circular cookie cutter to pull in the edges to form perfect circles. Let stand to cool and get crisp before removing from the baking sheets.

5 Put the chocolate in a heatproof bowl set over a saucepan of gently simmering water (make sure the bottom of the bowl does not touch the water) and stir until melted. Spread most of the chocolate onto a sheet of parchment paper. When the chocolate is at the point of setting, place the cookies flat-side down on the chocolate and let it harden completely.

6 Cut around the florentines and remove from the parchment paper. Spread a little more chocolate on the coated side of the florentines and use a fork to mark waves in the chocolate. Let stand to set. Keep cool.

Madeleines

Makes about 30

- ½ cup plus 2 tbsp (1¼ sticks) unsalted butter, melted and cooled, plus extra for greasing
- 3 eggs
- 1 egg yolk
- 1 tsp vanilla extract
- ¾ cup superfine sugar
- 1¼ cups all-purpose flour
- 1 tsp baking powder

1 Preheat the oven to 375°F/190°C. Lightly grease 30 cups in 2–3 standard madeleine pans.

2 Place the eggs, egg yolk, vanilla extract, and sugar in a large bowl and beat with a handheld electric mixer until very pale and thick.

3 Sift in the flour and baking powder and fold in lightly and evenly using a metal spoon. Fold in the melted butter evenly.

4 Spoon the batter into the prepared pans, filling to about three-quarters full. Bake in the preheated oven for 8–10 minutes, until risen and golden.

5 Remove the cakes carefully from the pans and cool on a wire rack. They are best served the day they are made.

Pistachio & Almond Tuiles

Makes about 6

- 1 egg white
- generous ¼ cup superfine sugar
- ¼ cup all-purpose flour
- ¼ cup pistachios, finely chopped
- ¼ cup ground almonds
- ½ tsp almond extract
- 3 tbsp unsalted butter, melted and cooled

1 Preheat the oven to 325°F/160°C. Line two baking sheets with parchment paper.

2 Whisk the egg white lightly with the sugar, then stir in the flour, pistachios, ground almonds, almond extract, and butter, mixing to a soft paste.

3 Place walnut-size spoonfuls of the mixture on the prepared baking sheets and use the back of the spoon to spread as thinly as possible. Bake in the preheated oven for 10–15 minutes, until pale golden.

4 Quickly lift each cookie with a spatula and place over the side of a rolling pin to shape into a curve. When set, transfer to a wire rack to cool.

Cream Palmiers

Makes 8

- ¼ cup granulated sugar
- 8 oz/225 g store-bought puff pastry

filling

- ⅔ cup heavy cream
- 1 tbsp confectioners' sugar, sifted
- few drops vanilla extract
- 2 tbsp strawberry jam

1 Preheat the oven to 425°F/220°C. Dust the work surface with half the granulated sugar and roll out the pastry on the sugared surface to a 10 x 12-inch/25 x 30-cm rectangle.

2 Sprinkle the rest of the sugar over the pastry and gently roll over it with the rolling pin. Roll the two short sides of the pastry into the center until they meet, moisten the edges that meet with a little water, and press together gently. Cut across the roll into 16 even slices.

3 Place the slices, cut-side down, on a dampened baking sheet. Use a rolling pin to flatten each one slightly.

4 Bake in the preheated oven for 15–18 minutes, until crisp and golden brown, turning the palmiers over halfway through cooking so that both sides caramelize. Transfer to a wire rack to cool.

5 For the filling, whip the cream, confectioners' sugar, and vanilla extract together until softly peaking. Sandwich the palmiers together with the jam and whipped cream and serve within 2–3 hours of filling.

Chocolate Éclairs

Makes 12

choux pastry
- 5 tbsp butter, cut into small pieces, plus extra for greasing
- ⅔ cup water
- ¾ cup all-purpose flour, sifted
- 2 eggs

pastry cream
- 2 eggs, beaten lightly
- ¼ cup superfine sugar
- 2 tbsp cornstarch
- 1¼ cups milk
- ¼ tsp vanilla extract

frosting
- 2 tbsp butter
- 1 tbsp milk
- 1 tbsp unsweetened cocoa
- ½ cup confectioners' sugar
- 1¾ oz/50 g white chocolate, broken into pieces

1 Preheat the oven to 400°F/200°C. Lightly grease a baking sheet.

2 For the pastry, place the water in a saucepan, add the butter, and heat gently until the butter melts. Bring to a rapid boil, then remove the pan from the heat and add the flour all at once, beating well until the mixture leaves the sides of the pan and forms a ball. Let cool slightly, then gradually beat in the eggs to form a smooth, glossy mixture. Spoon into a large pastry bag fitted with a ½-inch/1-cm plain tip.

3 Sprinkle the baking sheet with a little water. Pipe 12 éclairs 3 inches/7.5 cm long, spaced well apart. Bake for 30–35 minutes, or until crisp and golden. Make a small slit in the side of each éclair to let the steam escape. Let cool on a wire rack.

4 Meanwhile, make the pastry cream. Whisk the eggs and sugar until thick and creamy, then fold in the cornstarch. Heat the milk until almost boiling and pour onto the eggs, whisking. Transfer to the saucepan and cook over low heat, stirring until thick. Remove the pan from the heat and stir in the vanilla extract. Cover with parchment paper and let cool.

5 To make the frosting, melt the butter with the milk in a saucepan, remove from the heat, and stir in the unsweetened cocoa and sugar. Split the éclairs lengthwise and pipe in the pastry cream. Spread the frosting over the top of the éclair. Melt a little white chocolate in a heatproof bowl set over a saucepan of gently simmering water (make sure the bottom of the bowl does not touch the water), then spoon the chocolate frosting on top, swirl in, and let set.

Mixed Berry Tartlets

Makes 12

dough

- scant 1½ cups all-purpose flour, plus extra for dusting
- ¾ cup confectioners' sugar
- ⅔ cup ground almonds
- ½ cup (1 stick) butter
- 1 egg yolk
- 1 tbsp milk

filling

- 1 cup cream cheese
- confectioners' sugar, to taste, plus extra for dusting
- 12 oz/350 g fresh mixed berries, such as blueberries, raspberries, and small strawberries

1 To make the dough, sift the flour and confectioners' sugar into a bowl. Stir in the ground almonds. Add the butter and rub in until the mixture resembles breadcrumbs. Add the egg yolk and milk and work in with a palette knife, then mix with your fingers until the dough binds together. Wrap the dough in plastic wrap and let chill in the refrigerator for 30 minutes.

2 Preheat the oven to 400°F/200°C. On a lightly floured surface, roll out the dough and use to line 12 deep tartlet or individual brioche pans. Prick the bottoms. Press a piece of foil into each tartlet, covering the edges, and bake in the preheated oven for 10–15 minutes, or until light golden brown. Remove the foil and bake for an additional 2–3 minutes. Transfer to a wire rack to cool.

3 To make the filling, place the cream cheese and confectioners' sugar in a bowl and mix together. Place a spoonful of filling in each tart shell and arrange the berries on top. Dust with sifted confectioners' sugar and serve.